THE GREAT OUTDOORS

HIKING

Revised and Updated

by Kristin Thoennes Keller

Consultant:
Jennifer Tripp
Director of Development and Communications
North Country Trail Association

Capstone
press

Mankato, Minnesota

Edge Books are published by Capstone Press,
151 Good Counsel Drive, P.O. Box 669, Mankato, Minnesota 56002.
www.capstonepress.com

Library of Congress Cataloging-in-Publication Data
Thoennes Keller, Kristin.
    Hiking / by Kristin Thoennes Keller.—Rev. and updated.
    p. cm.—(Edge Books. The great outdoors)
    Includes bibliographical references and index.
    ISBN-13: 978-1-4296-0821-3 (hardcover)
    ISBN-10: 1-4296-0821-8 (hardcover)
    1. Hiking—Juvenile literature. 2. Hiking. I. Title. II. Series.
GV199.52.T46 2008
796.51—dc22   2007012261

Summary: Describes the equipment, skills, safety issues, and environmental concerns
    of hiking.

Editorial Credits
Carrie Braulick, editor; Katy Kudela, photo researcher; Tom Adamson, revised edition
    editor; Thomas Emery, revised edition designer; Kyle Grenz, revised edition
    production designer

Photo Credits
Capstone Press/Gary Sundermeyer, 7, 11, 17, 21, 23, 29, 31
Jeff Henry/Roche Jaune Pictures, Inc., 25, 33
Jeff March Nature Photography, 41
Jon Gnass/Gnass Photo Images, 35
Joseph Slabaugh, 44 (inset)
Kathy Adams Clark/KAC Productions, 38
Kent and Donna Dannen, 9
Photo Network/Henryk T. Kaiser, 14
Photri-Microstock/C. W. Biedel, M.D., 39 (top)
Rob and Ann Simpson, 42
Shutterstock/Jakub Cejpek, cover; Cynthia Burkhardt, 44 (background)
Tom Devol/Gnass Photo Images, 12
Unicorn Stock Photos/Rod Furgason, 36
Visuals Unlimited/Mark E. Gibson, 5; Mark S. Skalny, 19; Robert Gustafson,
    39 (bottom)

1 2 3 4 5 6 12 11 10 09 08 07

TABLE OF CONTENTS

Features ━━━━━━━━━━━━━━━━━━━━━━━━━━

Essential content terms are highlighted and are defined at the bottom of the page where they first appear.

Chapter 1

HIKING

Learn about different types of hiking, where to hike, and terrain.

From the woods to the mountains to the desert, anywhere is a great place to go hiking. Walking in the great outdoors allows you to slow down and enjoy the scenery. A long hike is also great exercise. Really long hikes up and down steep hills can also be a physical and mental challenge.

Recreational Hiking

Most people hike for recreation. Some hikers complete their hike in one day. This type of hiking is called day hiking.

Others go for a little more adventure. They carry camping equipment in backpacks to stay overnight outdoors. This activity is called backpacking.

Long-distance hikers take hiking to the extreme. These hikers walk hundreds or thousands of miles over several weeks in all kinds of weather.

Hiking is a popular way to get exercise in the
great outdoors.

Hiking Areas

Most hikers walk on trails. State and national parks provide trails for hikers. Nature centers and local governments also provide hiking trails. Some hiking organizations build and maintain their own trails.

The terrain on a hike can vary greatly. Hikers might encounter low, rolling hills. They might walk over sand in the desert. Loose, rocky terrain called scree covers many mountainsides and steep hills. Hikers have to be ready for anything.

EDGE FACT

The American Discovery Trail is a coast-to-coast, multiuse hiking trail that covers more than 6,800 miles (10,943 kilometers).

scree—small loose stones covering a hiking trail

6

Hiking
Club
Trail

Signs mark trails for hikers.

Chapter 2

EQUIPMENT

Learn about what to pack, safe drinking water, appropriate hiking clothing, and more.

Day hikes require much less equipment than backpacking and long-distance trips do. But hikers must think carefully about what they will need for the day. Hikers bring items that will keep them safe and comfortable.

Day Packs

Hikers should have a day pack. Day packs are usually made of nylon. This material is strong and water-resistant. Some hikers cover their day packs with waterproof nylon rain covers. These covers are coated with plastic to keep hikers' equipment dry in heavy rain.

water-resistant—material that resists water

Hikers wear day packs to carry their equipment.

Some hikers use day packs with an internal framesheet. This panel of hard plastic supports the pack. It makes packs more comfortable for hikers to carry. Most packs with an internal framesheet have stays. These stiff metal rods help the pack keep its shape.

Hikers' day packs should be large enough to carry all of their equipment. The packs are measured in cubic inches. Day packs should contain about 2,000 cubic inches (32,800 cubic centimeters) of space. They should have separate compartments. These compartments help hikers organize their gear.

EDGE FACT

In 2005, scientists announced that they had invented a backpack that generates its own electricity. It uses the hiker's walking movement to make enough energy to power several small electronic gadgets at once.

Hikers can adjust the straps on day packs to make them more comfortable to wear.

Hikers' day packs should be comfortable. The packs should weigh no more than one-fourth of the hikers' body weight. Many day packs have padded backs and straps. This feature makes the packs more comfortable to carry. Hikers should check the fit and weight of a loaded day pack before their hike.

Water and Food

Hikers must carry water. They should carry at least 1 quart (.95 liter) of water for every 5 miles (8 kilometers) they plan to hike. Hikers should stop often to drink water. They should drink before they become thirsty to prevent dehydration. People who are

dehydration—not having enough water in the body

dehydrated can become very sick. Hikers in extremely hot or cold weather should drink extra water.

Some hikers plan to walk near natural water sources such as streams or ponds. These hikers carry less water with them. Instead, they carry equipment to purify water from natural sources.

Water can be purified a few different ways. Some hikers carry a water filter. Others use iodine tablets, crystals, or drops to treat water. Water can also simply be boiled in a pan for three to five minutes to purify it.

Hikers should bring food to help them maintain their energy levels. Hikers should stop every one or two hours to eat. High-energy food, such as beef jerky or peanuts, are great for hiking.

EDGE FACT

Using iodine tablets is an easy way to purify water. But they make the water taste bad.

A compass can help guide hikers as they travel.

Maps

Hikers should have a map of the area where they are hiking. Many parks and hiking organizations have maps of trails. Most of these are topographical maps. They show an area's surface features. These features include rivers and mountains. The maps have curving lines to show the height of certain areas.

topographical map—a map that shows the land's features and how steep or flat the land is

14

Other Tools

Other equipment is handy to have on a hiking trip. Some additional items are necessary for emergencies or unexpected situations.

- **Firestarter or Waterproof Matches**—to keep warm, signal others, or to cook; keep these items in a waterproof container

- **Flashlight**—with new batteries

- **Pocketknife**—to alert others, cut a bandage, or untie a knot

- **First Aid Kit**—to take care of minor injuries

- **Compass**—to know what direction you are heading

- **Global Positioning System (GPS)**—uses satellites in space to help people locate their position

- **Hiking Sticks**—for support and balance on rough terrain

EDGE FACT

A new game associated with hiking is called geocaching. Hikers use a GPS device to find caches that others have hidden. It's like searching for hidden treasure!

Clothing

Most people hike during seasons of mild weather. But the temperature often changes throughout the day. Hikers should dress in layers. They can add or remove layers depending on the weather.

Hikers prefer a synthetic fabric for the layer of clothing next to the skin. Polypropylene draws moisture away from the skin.

Hikers should not wear cotton clothing, such as jeans. Cotton dries slowly. It can make hikers cold and uncomfortable.

Fleece makes a good middle layer of clothing. It's lightweight but warm.

Hikers' top layer of clothing should be windproof and water-resistant. Many hikers wear nylon jackets and polypropylene pants.

Some hikers bring a breathable nylon waterproof jacket in case of heavy rain. Jackets that are not breathable should have slits to allow air to pass through. It's also smart to bring a change of clothing.

synthetic—made by people rather than found in nature

Many hikers bring a mixture of foods called gorp on their hikes. This mixture provides energy for hikers. Some people say gorp stands for "granola, oatmeal, raisins, and peanuts." Others say it stands for "good old raisins and peanuts."

Ingredients:

1 cup almonds
1 cup banana chips
1 cup cashews
2 cups toasted oat cereal
1 cup chopped dates
1 small package of
   dried apples
1 cup figs
1 cup macadamia nuts

1 cup coated chocolate candies
1 cup oatmeal
1 cup peanuts
1 cup pecans
1 cup prunes
1 cup raisins
1 cup shredded coconut
1 cup sunflower seeds
1 cup walnuts

Equipment:

Large bowl
Large spoon
Plastic bags or containers

1. Combine all ingredients in a large bowl.

2. Mix ingredients together with a large spoon.

3. Divide into plastic bags or containers for packing.

Footwear

Hikers need proper footwear. Hiking boots have thick soles and deep grooves to help hikers grip surfaces. Hikers choose boots that fit comfortably. Shoes that are too tight can cause hikers' feet to become sore.

Experienced hikers usually wear wool socks or socks made of synthetic fabric blends. They do not wear cotton socks. Hikers' feet will probably get sweaty. Cotton stays wet. The wet material will rub against the skin and cause blisters on hikers' feet. Some hikers wear thin liner socks made of polyester and nylon to soak up moisture.

Outdoor Protection

Insects are common in hiking areas. Hikers should frequently apply insect repellent to their clothing to help prevent bites. Long-sleeved shirts, pants, and a hat can also protect hikers from insect bites. Many hikers tuck their pants into their socks.

EDGE FACT

In 2001, people spent more than $18 billion on outdoor gear, clothing, footwear, and other hiking gear.

Hiking boots are sturdy and have grooves to help hikers grip surfaces.

Hikers need sun protection. They should apply sunscreen to their skin to prevent sunburn. Hikers often wear sunglasses to protect their eyes. Many hikers wear a hat to shade their face.

Dogs

Some people hike with their dogs. They may attach small packs filled with hiking equipment to their dogs.

Hikers should properly care for their dogs. They should keep their dogs leashed and make sure dogs are allowed in the area. Hikers should bring extra water and food for their dogs.

EDGE FACT

Make sure your dog is in good enough shape for a hike. He might have to start out with short hikes at first until he gets used to all that walking.

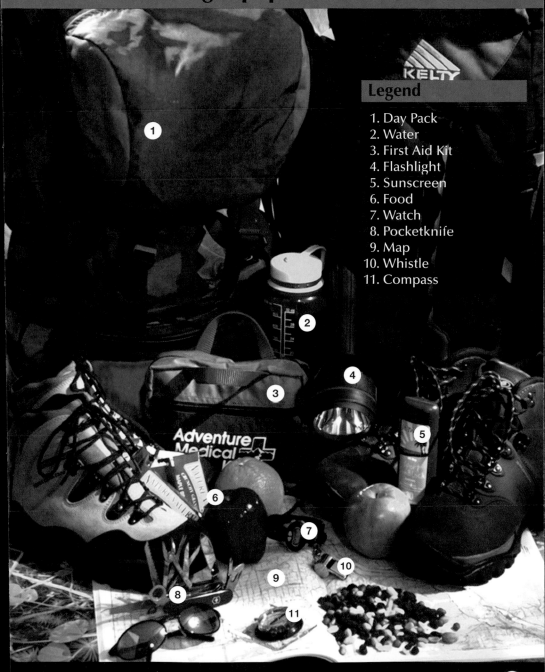

Essential Hiking Equipment

Legend

1. Day Pack
2. Water
3. First Aid Kit
4. Flashlight
5. Sunscreen
6. Food
7. Watch
8. Pocketknife
9. Map
10. Whistle
11. Compass

Chapter 3

SKILLS AND TECHNIQUES

Learn about preparing for a hike, hiking terrain, and topographical maps.

Experienced hikers carefully plan their hikes. They look at a map of the hiking area. They find out about the area's weather and know the forecast. Hikers also decide how difficult of a hike to take.

Hiking Time

Hikers should plan the length of their hike. They should return before dark. Hikers usually allow about 30 minutes for each mile (1.6 kilometers) that they hike. They allow 30 additional minutes for every 1,000 feet (300 meters) of elevation.

Hiking up hills is more difficult than walking on flat land. Hikers adjust hiking times according to their skill level. Even a moderate hike with an elevation gain of 1,000 feet (300 meters) can feel like climbing 1,000 stairs all at once.

elevation—the height of the land

Hikers should check a map before they begin their trip.

Most hikers allow extra time for the return trip. Hikers might walk slower during the return hike because they are tired.

Stretching

Hikers should stretch before, during, and after hikes. Stretching can help prevent injuries and sore muscles. Hikers stretch far enough to feel a gentle pull. They should hold a stretch for about 30 to 60 seconds.

Hikers stretch various body parts. They stretch their legs and lower back. They also stretch their shoulders, neck, arms, and chest.

Terrain

Hikers choose terrain based on their skill and fitness level. Beginning hikers should choose flat terrain or low hills. This type of terrain usually is easy for hikers to walk on.

Steep hills and mountainsides are more challenging. Hikers' feet and knees can quickly become tired. Hikers on hills and mountainsides sometimes walk on

Steep, rocky areas may be a challenge for hikers.

switchback trails. These trails follow a zigzag pattern to make it easier for hikers to grip surfaces. On steep slopes, hikers should take small steps. They should keep their knees relaxed and bent while they hike down steep slopes. These practices help relieve pressure on hikers' legs.

Reading Topographical Maps

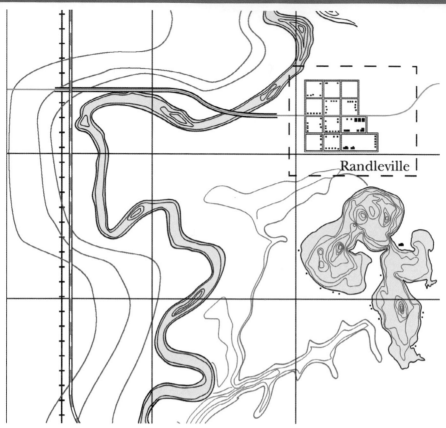

Randleville

Contour Line
Primary Highway
Secondary Highway
Railroad
Bridge
Water
House

Like other maps, topographical maps show features such as rivers, roads, and buildings. But they also use contour lines to show the land's elevation. Widely spaced lines or areas of no lines show level ground. Closely spaced lines show steep slopes.

Hiking—Skills and Techniques

Scree can cause hikers to slip. Hikers on this terrain should move slowly and watch where they step.

River gorges can pose dangers to hikers. These deep valleys are located at the sides of rivers. Gorges have steep, rocky sides and loose gravel. Hikers should not hike in a river gorge during heavy rainfall. The river can rise quickly.

Hikers sometimes need to cross streams. Walk carefully when crossing streams. The rocks you step on are probably wet and slippery. Hikers should only cross streams that are moving slowly. They should look for a wide spot in the stream and cross at an angle moving upstream. These practices help hikers keep their balance.

Hikers should not cross rivers. Rivers are often deep and may have strong currents.

contour lines—curving lines on a map that show the shape of the land

Chapter 4

RESPONSIBLE HIKING

Learn about staying on the trail, keeping the trail clean, and respecting wildlife.

Hikers can cause problems in some hiking areas. Overused trails often erode. The soil on these trails wears away. Hikers sometimes trample plants and harm them. Some hiking areas are becoming polluted. But responsible hikers know how to take care of the environment.

Trails

Responsible hikers stay on the trail as much as possible. They walk single file to keep the trail at its original width. They do not wander off the trail. Hikers who leave the trail can destroy plants growing near the trail.

Hikers may need to step off the trail in certain situations. For example, they may need to allow people on horseback to pass.

erode—to wear away or destroy little by little

Responsible hikers pick up trash that they find along trails.

Hikers may take breaks off the trail. Other hikers then can continue to use the trail. For breaks, hikers should choose areas where they will cause the least amount of damage. Rocky areas or places without plants are best for breaks.

Hikers often meet other hikers on the trail. Responsible hikers move off to one side of the trail when this happens. They stop walking to let others pass.

Respecting the Environment

Hikers should care for the environment. They take any trash they create with them. They can dispose of the trash after their hike. Hikers should use resealable packages for food. They should carry water and other beverages in plastic bottles. These bottles can be sealed and reused.

EDGE FACT

Some trails are multiuse. Horses, mountain bikes, and even four-wheelers are allowed on some trails. You should know on what type of trail you're hiking.

Hikers can take breaks on large rocks near the trail to prevent damage to plants.

Responsible hikers care for the environment in other ways. They pick up and carry out trash they see along trails. They avoid picking flowers and taking other items found in nature home with them. Members of hiking organizations may add soil to eroded trails to maintain them.

Respecting Wildlife

Animals live in many hiking areas. They usually stay away from busy trails. But hikers might see some wildlife on their hikes. Hikers should respect animals' need for food, water, and shelter. Responsible hikers observe animals from behind cover and at a distance. They do not approach animals. This behavior may threaten the animals or scare them away.

Many animals have young during spring. Hikers should be especially respectful during this season. Animals may be more aggressive in spring to protect their young.

Hikers use binoculars to watch wildlife from a distance.

Responsible hikers do not scatter food or feed animals. Animals might become used to finding food on trails and lose their natural fear of people. Some of these animals may become aggressive. For example, bears that people feed may try to force food away from people.

Chapter 5

SAFETY

Learn about winter hiking, harmful plants, and harmful critters.

Responsible hikers prepare for unexpected situations. They tell someone where they will be hiking. Beginning hikers should walk with at least one other person. The other person can get help if an emergency occurs. Hikers should have basic first aid skills to treat injuries. Hikers should always carry a cell phone.

Weather Safety

Hikers should pay attention to the weather forecast before they begin their hike. They should not hike if thunderstorms are predicted. Hikers should look for signs of approaching storms. For example, they watch the direction in which clouds are moving. A thunderstorm may be approaching if clouds are moving in different directions. Hikers may notice the wind die down or feel a sudden rush of cold air before a thunderstorm begins.

Hikers should know how to use the items in their first aid kits.

Hikers who are caught outside during storms should stay away from water sources, tall trees, cliffs, and ridges. Lightning is more likely to strike in these places. Heavy rain can make many hiking areas slippery. Hikers should be careful when they hike after rainfall.

Winter Hiking

Some people hike in winter or during cold weather. These hikers should make sure to keep themselves warm. They need to wear warm clothing such as hats, mittens, scarves, and heavy coats. They should be careful not to become chilled or soaked with sweat. These conditions can cause hypothermia. This condition occurs when a person's body temperature becomes too low. People with hypothermia can become confused and sleepy. They could even die.

Winter hikers also must prevent frostbite. This condition occurs when cold temperatures cause the skin to freeze. These hikers should wear layers of warm clothing that cover their whole bodies. They may protect their face with a ski mask.

Many winter hikers wear a waterproof outside layer of clothing. It's important that hikers' skin remain dry. Wet skin freezes more quickly than dry skin does.

EDGE FACT

Hikers need about 1,000 more calories per day in winter than during other seasons.

Harmful Plants

Poison ivy, poison oak, and poison sumac are three common harmful plants in North America. These plants release an oil that causes a rash to form on the skin. The oil spreads easily. Hikers should learn to recognize and avoid these plants.

Many hikers wear long pants and long-sleeved shirts to protect themselves from poison ivy, oak, and sumac. Hikers wash their hands and clothes immediately after their hikes. Rashes begin 48 to 72 hours after contact with the skin. People can use creams to help relieve the itching.

Poison Ivy

Poison ivy usually grows along a red vine. The vines often grow up tree trunks. But poison ivy may form an upright bush if it has nothing to cling to. Poison ivy leaves grow in clusters of three. The middle leaf is larger than the outer two. The leaves are red in the spring and shiny green in late spring and summer. The leaves turn orange or red in the fall. The edges of the leaves can be smooth or jagged. Poison ivy grows throughout most of the United States and southern Canada.

Poison Oak

Poison oak shares many of poison ivy's features. But poison oak almost always grows as a bush. It is usually about 3 feet (.9 meter) tall. Poison oak's leaves are lobe-shaped. They have rounded notches on their sides. A hairlike growth often covers the plant's leaves, trunk, and berries. Poison oak grows throughout most of the United States and southern Canada.

Poison Sumac

Poison sumac is a large shrub. It can grow as tall as 12 feet (3.6 meters). The plant is green during spring and summer. It turns yellow or red during fall. Pairs of leaves grow opposite one another along a single stem. These leaves may grow up to about 1 foot (.3 meter) long. The top of the stem has a single leaf. One stem usually has seven to 13 leaves. Poison sumac grows best in wet, swampy areas. Poison sumac is common in and around Michigan in the Great Lakes area. It also is common on the southeastern coast of the United States.

Animal Safety

Hikers should know how to stay safe around animals. Hikers may encounter other hikers' dogs on trails. These hikers should give the dogs room to pass. Hikers with dogs should control their animals.

Hikers should learn what types of wild animals live in the area. They need to learn how to stay safe around these animals. For example, hikers should back up slowly and look to the side if they encounter a bear at close range. Hikers in areas where venomous snakes are common should only put their hands and feet where they can see them. Snakes sometimes lie underneath rocks or logs. They might strike if they are startled.

Many hikers warn animals of their presence. They talk to others as they walk. They may hum or call out. Hikers may tie small bells to their packs. Some hikers occasionally thump the ground with a hiking stick to warn snakes of their presence.

venomous—snakes that produce a toxic substance and pass it into a victim's body through a bite

Tick Safety

Hikers should try to prevent tick bites. Wood ticks and deer ticks are common in North America. Wood ticks cause Rocky Mountain spotted fever. This disease causes headaches, muscle aches, and fever. It can also cause a rash on the palms of the hands and soles of the feet. The rash can spread to other parts of the body. Serious cases can cause death.

tick—a small blood-sucking insect that attaches itself to animals and people

Deer ticks cause Lyme disease. This disease causes a target-shaped rash around the tick bite. Symptoms of Lyme disease include fever, headache, and muscle soreness.

Hikers should check themselves often for ticks. They may wear tick repellent. Hikers can wear long-sleeved shirts and pants to prevent ticks from reaching the skin.

Safety When Lost

Hikers pay attention to the trail as they walk. They should look for landmarks such as large rocks. Hikers need to stay calm and look for familiar landmarks if they do become lost. They should stay in one place and blow a whistle to alert others.

Groups of hikers may decide on a whistle code. For example, a group may decide two long whistle blows means that someone is lost.

Traffic Safety

Hikers sometimes must walk on roadways with traffic. These hikers should walk single file toward oncoming traffic. They should wear brightly colored clothing to help drivers see them.

Safe hikers prevent accidents and are prepared if an accident does occur. These hikers make their outings more enjoyable for themselves and others.

Scott Rogers hiked the entire Appalachian Trail.

The Bionic Hiker

EDGE FACT

The Appalachian Trail runs more than 2,000 miles (3,220 kilometers) through the Appalachian Mountains in the eastern United States.

44

On May 25, 1998, a hunting accident changed Scott Rogers' life forever. He was shot in the left leg, which was amputated above the knee. Scott received a high-tech artificial leg. He decided to fulfill a lifelong dream to hike the Appalachian Trail.

Scott began his long hike on March 22, 2004. Newspapers and TV stations reported on his progress. People started calling him the "Bionic Hiker." Things were going well, but Scott had to stop when his brother Barry died. He returned home to be with his family. He knew he'd be back, though. Scott finished the Appalachian Trail on September 21, 2005.

Scott still likes hiking. He also speaks around the country about his experience. He tells people how important it is to never give up and have faith that they can do anything.

GLOSSARY

dehydration (dee-hye-DRAY-shuhn)—the condition that occurs when the body does not have enough water

elevation (el-uh-VAY-shuhn)—the height of the land above sea level

erode (e-RODE)—to gradually wear away

iodine (EYE-uh-dine)—a chemical element that is used to kill germs

purify (PYOOR-uh-fye)—to make something clean

synthetic (sin-THET-ik)—something that is made by people rather than found in nature

terrain (tuh-RAYN)—the surface of the ground

venomous (VEN-uhm-us)—able to produce a toxic substance called venom

READ MORE

Loy, Jessica. *Follow the Trail: A Young Person's Guide to the Great Outdoors.* New York: Holt, 2003.

Slade, Suzanne. *Let's Go Hiking.* Adventures Outdoors. New York: PowerKids Press, 2007.

Wilson, Jef. *Hiking for Fun!* For Fun! Minneapolis: Compass Point Books, 2006.

INTERNET SITES

FactHound offers a safe, fun way to find Internet sites related to this book. All of the sites on FactHound have been researched by our staff.

Here's how:

1. Visit *www.facthound.com*
2. Choose your grade level.
3. Type in this book ID **1429608218** for age-appropriate sites. You may also browse subjects by clicking on letters, or by clicking pictures and words.
4. Click on the **Fetch It** button.

FactHound will fetch the best sites for you!

INDEX